Love Them Enough to Pull Them out of the Fire

Deborah Woodfork

Love Them Enough to Pull Them out of the Fire
PUBLISHED BY FAITHWALK PRESS
2426 Bragg Boulevard
Fayetteville NC 20303

Unless otherwise indicated, Scripture quotations are taken from the Holman RainBow Study Bible (HRSB) copyright 1993.Use by permission. Scripture quotations marked (KJV)

Published in the United States by FAITHWALK PRESS

First Edition
ISBN-13:978-1544614687
ISBN-10:1544614683

Table of Contents

Introduction

Sometimes in life, we sit and wonder about the things that are taking place around the world today.

Some are good and some are bad, but we, as Christians, know that these things must come to pass. That's why it is very important for us as believers to move forward in our work in the vineyard. We must let the world know that Jesus is real, hell is real, and heaven is real.

Are we must ask ourselves, do we know who Jesus is? This book of love will help you know Jesus, and believe God and His word. This book will show you that He loves us and He wants the best for us.

Deborah Woodfork

Jeremiah 29:11

For I know the thoughts that I think toward you saith the Lord, thoughts of peace, and not of evil, to give you an expected end.

It's possible that you all can get together as a group and share Gods love and the vineyard's work.

Chapter 1: Everyone Needs to Know Jesus

Each day the Saints who love God, and who have in their hearts the desire to fast and pray, go out in God's vineyard to feed His sheep and tell them about Jesus. To tell them that Jesus loves them and that He is coming back again.

Matthew 9:37-38

---

[37]Then saith He unto His disciples, The harvest truly is plenteous, but the labourers are few; [38]Pray ye therefore the Lord of the harvest, that He will send forth labourers into His harvest.

Matthew 20:1

For the kingdom of heaven is like unto a man that is an householder, which went out early in the morning to hire laborers into His vineyard.

Let us pray together. Love together. Reach out together. Let us be honest with ourselves. The message is for the Saints that have a heart's desire to save God's people and to work together as brothers and sisters for God. There is work to be done because Jesus is coming. Jesus is coming. Jesus is *coming.*

Chapter 2: How Can You Love without Loving?

The definition of loving is feeling or showing love or great care. The definition of love is an intense feeling of deep affection. Don't get me wrong, both are of God. There is a difference in them, but one without the other won't work.

How can we love without loving? That heart-to-heart loving. That hand-to-hand loving. That is what you call loving. We must always show the real love of God.

It is a blessing to be able to have a home to live in. It is a blessing to have food to eat. It is a blessing to have water to drink and water to take a bath. These blessings are all because of the grace of God and His Son Jesus Christ.

It is also a blessing to be able to provide funds for programs to help the homeless have a place to sleep and food to eat. I say amen, Saints. Sometimes working with a program in an organization is good. These things are good, but they have a time in which they can show love. When the program time is over, what's next? The homeless are still in the cold without knowing where to stay. Your giving is important.

Anybody can stay inside the wall and work. It takes the power of God to stand for the vineyard to work. This world was built on love, and if you are giving for any other reason, your giving is in vain. We look to see if everyone else is loving, but we must search our own hearts and minds.

Matthew 7:3

And why beholdest thou the mote that is in thy brother's eye, but considerest not the beam that is in thine own eye?

Proverbs 11:30

The fruit of the righteous is a tree of life, And he that winneth souls is wise.

These homeless are still in need because their minds need to know about Jesus. When they get a touch of Jesus they will never need a helping hand again. It is time for us as believers to make sure they know about Jesus so they will have a choice to live for Him.

Even movie stars need Jesus, too. The enemy doesn't care how much money you have. It can't buy you Salvation. I know they are crying out for Jesus but there is no one to hear their cry. They are human, too. Most of them were singing for God before the enemy came to decide their minds. That's why you see some of them dying, trying to reach out to the world of believers, but no one is there to stand for them.

We need to pray with them the prayer that Jesus told us to pray. Jesus said to pray after this manner:

Matthew 6:9-13

---

[9]After this manner therefore pray ye: Our Father which art in heaven, Hallowed be they name.

[10]Thy kingdom come. Thy will be done in earth, as it is in heaven.

[11]Give us this day our daily bread.

¹²And forgive us our debts, as we forgive our debtors.

¹³And lead us not into temptation, but deliver us from evil: For thine is the kingdom, and the power, and glory, forever. Amen.

If we only knew how powerful that prayer is, and that all we need. How bless we would be.

We must share the Book of Life like God said to do because God can save them; look how He saves us. The only way to stop God's homeless from sleeping in the cold of winter and the heat of summer without shelter is that we must get out there where they are and lead them to Christ.

Then, they won't be holding up a sign at the red light. There won't be anyone there anymore. Their soul has met with Jesus.

Chapter 3: Let's Prepare for the Vineyard

Why do you think God chose you to be a blessing to them? Come to the vineyard and then you will know if you have done all God commanded you to do. Their minds needs to be renewed. Take time and love them the right way. All they are wanting to see the love of God on the Saint's faces; then you will see that smile on their faces. You will see their eyes open up when they see your face, and they will start talking as if they haven't talked in years.

Did you know that these people are the next teachers, preachers, and lawyers? That's why it's important to take your gift to them with your own hands.

Hosea 4:6

My people are destroyed for the lack of knowledge: because thou hast rejected knowledge, I will also reject thee, that thou shalt be no priest to me: seeing thou hast forgotten the law of thy God, I will also forget thy children.

Jesus already knew we were going to need the Holy Ghost's power to do the vineyard's work. When Jesus was out in the vineyard, He was concerned about one thing, for them to be born again and to renew their minds.

The Samaritan woman had five husbands. If Jesus had not met her in the vineyard, telling her about that living water, she would have been looking to marry yet another man. But she met Jesus and He told her about that living water and said that if she would drink that water she would never thirst again. That living water is Jesus. Saints, let's take Jesus to those that thirst. They don't really want the money; they use it to buy strong drinks and buy drugs. They want you to bring them some peace of mind. That peace of mind only comes though knowing Jesus.

Galatians 2:20

I am crucified with Christ: nevertheless I live; yet not I, but Christ liveth in me: and the life which I now live in the flesh I live by faith of the Son of God, who loves me, and gave himself for me.

We ourselves know, being a Christians, how the enemy tries to mess with our minds. How we have to fight the enemy with the word of God. Just think about the lost that don't have God's word. I can't imagine what they're going through without Jesus.

Look how the grace of God lets us get up every morning and read our Bible. Not because you have an education, or a degree, or lots of money: but because we have God's grace all around us.

1 Corinthians 13:3

And though I bestow all my goods to feed the poor, and though I give my body to be burned, and have not charity, it profiteth me nothing.

We must do the vineyard as one whole body how and where we are going to take the next step for Christ. God's love should always want us to be a giver. Always be really to give love to each other.

John 3:17

For God sent not His Son into the world, to condemn the world; but that the world through Him might be saved.

With the love of God in our heart, let us start loving not just love. Then, perhaps someday we might ride down the street and not see a single homeless person in sight.

Ezekiel 3:18

When I say to a wicked, Thou shalt surely die; and thou givest him not warning, nor speakest to warn the wicked from his wicked way, to save his life; the same wicked man shall die in his iniquity; but his blood will I require at thine hand.

I see that the vineyard is empty. We say that we love God and His people, but we don't show it. Faith without works is dead. God is tired of people just talking, trying to save people who are already saved. He wants you in the vineyard where work is needed. If Saints start taking God's word to the vineyard together in love, then when you come together as the church to worship with one another, you can have true worship. God is saying to the church, "it is time be the church."

Unfortunately, the churches are just beating each other up. I believe that's the reason the unbelievers don't want to go into the church today. The Saints are acting like the world and looking like the world. God is telling us to put away all these things of the world, things such as not loving one another, gossiping, adultery, fornicating, lying—everything that is sinful. The things of this world shouldn't matter to believers. God wants us to think about our lives because of immorality, impurity, passion, evil desire, and greed—which amounts to idolatry. Yes! All these diseases in the world today come from lack of love and sin. The bible says fornication is a sin, and that committing adultery, marrying the same sex is a sin. In these last days let us be honest with ourselves: disobedience and the lack of love are keeping God's people apart. For it is because of these things that the wrath of God will come upon the sons of disobedience.

I tell you that some sad day are coming here on this earth. The Sodom and Gomorrah days are all around us. We thought AIDS was the worst disease we had ever seen. But what's coming to be is a disease and the name is sin—. Because God said the wages of sin is death. But the gift of God is eternal life. How will the world know sin death if there are no Saints are in the vineyard?

James 4:7

Submit yourselves therefore to God. Resist the devil, and he will flee from you.

Saints of God, everywhere you go people are giving themselves titles, putting themselves in the pulpit, building churches out of any building and anywhere. People of God are missing the revelation, trying to build, building to worship—when the real worship is Love. Let us stop looking for buildings and start looking for Jesus in the vineyard. God is calling for a true church because He is coming back soon. He wants the love in the hearts of men, so let us stop wasting the time we have left, worrying about who has the biggest church and who has the most members. It's not about denomination. There are many denominations but there is one God. Let us put aside our denominations, pick up the true and living God and go out in the vineyard. It's about Jesus, so go tell your neighbor about how Jesus can save them and set them free.

1 Corinthians 3:16-17

---

[16]Know ye not that ye are the temple of God, and that the Spirit of God dwelleth in you?
[17]If any man defile the temple of God, him shall God destroy; for the temple of God is holy, which temple ye are.

So let us stop fighting about the color of our skin. God is not of color He is of sprint. There is a mystery in why all of Gods children are not the same color. Only God knows and the only way to complete Gods command is to Love.

John 3:16

For God so love the world, that He gave His only begotten Son, that whosoever believer in Him should not perish, But have everlasting life.

God loves the whole world. That means He gave His life not for the color of His skin. But for Sin.

Jesus already knew that heaven is not made up of hate, or color of your skin, or your race, or how rich or poor you are. It's time to stand up for Jesus, and stop trying to fault one another, and being jealous of one another.

Song of Solomon 8:6

Set me as a seal upon thine heart; as a seal Upon thine arm: for love is as strong as death; and jealousy is cruel as the grave: the coal therefore is coals of fire which hath a most vehement flame.

13

We also give up too quickly. We are going to have to love until the end. Stay out in the vineyard together until Jesus comes.

Remember 9/11? We were out in the vineyard for a little while, but we stopped and came back inside. Remember the Church in Charleston, S.C. where the nine Saints were killed? We went out to gather in the vineyard for a little while. Again, we came back inside the walls. The Bible says pray without ceasing. Saints, if we pray together and stay together we can stand, and we will stand, and we will love.

2 Timothy 4:1-5

[1]I charge thee therefore before God, And the Lord Jesus Christ, who shall judge the quick and the dead at His appearing and His kingdom;
[2]Preach the word; be instant in season, out of season; reprove, rebuke, exhort with all long suffering and doctrine.
[3]For the time will come when they will not endure sound doctrine; but after their own lusts shall they harp to themselves. Teachers, having itching ears;
[4]And they shall turn away their ears from the truth, and shall be turned unto fables.
[5]But watch thou in all things, endure afflictions, do the work of an evangelist, make full proof of thy ministry.

You may feel uncomfortable with other Saints, but sometimes you must come out your comfort zone and get in the love-in-faith zone. It doesn't matter if you are Baptist, Methodist, Holiness, or Jehovah's Witness, black or white. God still requires you to love one another.

Matthew 11:29

Take my yoke upon you, and learn of me; for I am meek and lowly in heart: and ye shall find rest unto your souls.

Don't think you are better than the unbeliever in the vineyard. It's time to show the Godly love. For the Saints that know the true and loving God share and preach the truth. The true word of God is clean, and will wash the dirt out of our lives.

Don't look back. Looking back is a set up for the devil. It is so that you can't see were God has brought you from. God deserve the praise for what He has done for His children. But, just look at Jesus and the things He had to endure which did not stop Him from going on the cross.

Titus 1:10-13

[10]For there are many unruly and vain talkers and deceivers, specially they of the circumcision:

15

[11]Whose mouths be stopped, who subvert whole houses, teaching things which they ought not, for filthy lucre's sake.
[12]One of themselves, even a prophet of their own, said, The Creations are always liars, evil beasts, and slow bellies.
[13]This witness is true. Wherefore rebuke them sharply, that they may be sound in the faith;

Titus 1:16

They profess that they know God; but in works they deny him, being abominable, and disobedient, and unto every good work reprobate.

Don't let the enemy stop you from going out in the vineyard just because some people are different. Our relationship with God is the only thing that matters.

We are helpmates to each other. We need each other. Stop talking about our differences and be about our Father's business.

Romans 14:13

Let us not therefore judge one another any-more: but judge this rather, that no man put a stumbling block or an occasion to fall and brother's way.

I want to ask you all, Believers, do you really believe? We teach the bible. We read the bible, but do we believe what God is saying about love and about the vineyard? The unbelievers are looking to the church. You must be pure and Holy. God is calling for holiness. If we listen, obey, and pray, God will heal this land. Look at the book of Jonah. Just know how God was always sending people out because that's there the work was needed.

Jonah 1:1-3

---

¹Now the word of the Lord came to Jonah son of Amittai: saying,
²Arise, go to Nineveh, that great city, and cry against it; for their wickedness is come up before me.
³But Jonah rose up to flee unto Tarshish from the presence of the Lord, and went down to Joppa; and he found a ship going Tarshish: so he paid the fare thereof, and went into it, to go with them unto Tarshish from the presence of the lord.

Jonah 3:1-5

---

¹And the word of the Lord came unto Jonah the second time, saying,
²Arise, go unto Nineveh, that great city, and preach unto it the preaching that I bid thee.
³So Jonah arose , and went unto Nineveh, according to the word of the Lord. Now Nineveh was an exceeding great city of three days' journey.

⁴And Jonah began to enter into the city a day's journey, and he cried, and said, Yet forty days, and Nineveh shall be overthrown.
⁵So the people of Nineveh believed God and proclaimed a fast, and put on sackcloth, from the greatest of them even to the least of them.

Jonah 3:10

And God saw their works, - that they had turned from their evil ways; –and God repented of evil, that He had said that He would do unto them; and He did it not.

Elijah was another great prophet that God used in the vineyard to do miracles. The prophet Elijah did sixteen miracles. He called the people to make a decision concerning God and he challenged the prophets of Baal to a fiery test. Elijah's Hebrew name means: my God is Jehovah.

Elias was another man that God command to go to the vineyard.

James 5:17-18

¹⁷Elias was subject to like passion as we are, and he prayed earnestly that it might not rain: and it rained not on the earth by the space of three years and six months.

[18]And he prayed again, and the heaven gave rain, and the earth brought forth her fruit.

Elias prayed earnestly and God heard Him and answered his prayer. God will hear and answer our prayer if we obey His word. There is healing and there is forgiveness of sin in praying. That's why God said to pray without ceasing because we can't do anything without *prayer.*

Daniel 6:26-28

[26]I make a decree, that in all the dominion of my kingdom men are to fear and tremble before the God of Daniel:
"For He is the living God,
and enduring forever, and
His kingdom is one which will not be destroyed,
and His dominion shall be ever unto the end.
[27]He delivereth and rescueth,
and He worketh signs and wonders
In heaven and on earth,
who hath delivered Daniel?
from the power of the lions."
[28]So this Daniel prospered in the reign of Darius, and the reign of Cyrus the Persian.

Daniel knew that God was not dead, that He was a living God. And he trusted God. We have to put our trust in God.

God is telling the Saints the same thing—to get up! And He has told us over and over many times to tell His people about His love, how He can save them from their sins. Look how the people accepted God as soon as Jonah got there, and told them to repent. God will heal this land. The vineyard is waiting.

Revelation 2:7

He that hath an ear, let him hear what the Spirit saith unto the churches; To him that overcometh will I give to eat of the tree of life, which is in the midst of the paradise of God."

Proverbs 11:30

The fruit of righteous is a tree of life; and he that winneth souls is wise.

Fellowship is what we do together as believers. Hospitality is how we show love to unbelievers. It's as if Jesus is looking around this world in saying "Where are the orphans? The people are struggling? The people who are broken? This is so powerful—to invite the homeless, the broken, those struggling, the orphans in and show them some love. God wants us to make room, Saints, at the table for *the sinners and the needy.*

Luke 14:16-17

---

¹⁶Then said unto him, "A certain man made a great supper, and bade many:
¹⁷And sent his servant at the suffer time to say to them that were bidden, Come; for all things are now ready."

Luke 14:21

---

²¹So that servant came, and shewed his lord these things. Then the master of the house being angry said to his servant, Go out quickly into the streets and lanes of the city, and bring in hither the poor, and the maimed, and the halt, and blind.
²²And the servant said, "Lord, it is done as thou hast commanded, and yet there is room."
²³And the lord said unto the servant, "Go out into the highways and hedges, and compel them to come in, that my house may be filled.
²⁴For I say unto you, That none of those men which were bidden shall taste of my supper."

Luke 14:12-14:

---

¹²Then said he also to him that bade him, "When thou makest a dinner or a supper, call not thy friends, nor thy brethren, neither thy kinsmen, nor thy rich

neighbours; lest they also bid thee again, and a recompence be made thee.

¹³But when thou makest a feast, call the poor, the maimed, the lame, the blind:

¹⁴And thou shalt be blessed; for they cannot recompense thee: for thou shalt be recompensed at the resurrection of the just."

They were making excuses to avoid coming to sit at the Master's table to eat and fellowship with the unbeliever. They rejected the call of the Master, but there are people in the street and by the highways are waiting for someone who knows Christ to invite them to the table to eat and to know Jesus.

In these recent days the churches are preaching on tithing and offering before telling the people about Jesus—that He saves and He delivers and He sets free. That's the first thing has to happen because without that nothing else matters. If you tell them about Jesus, and they accept Him into their lives, you won't have to preach every Sunday about tithing. They will give and they will be cheerful givers.

1 Peter 5:1-2

[1]The elder which are among you I exhort, who am also an elder and witness of our sufferings of Christ, and also a partaker of the glory that shall be revealed. [2]Feed the flock of God which is among you, taking the oversight there of, not by constraint, but willingly: not for filthy lucre, but of a readily mind.

He wants us to love His flocks in the vineyard. He also wants us to be examples to the flocks.

Revelation 7:17

For the lamb which is in the midst of the throne shall feed them, and shall lead them unto living fountains of water: and God shall wipe away all tears from their eyes.

Chapter 4: The Assurance of Christ to the Saints: God Has Your Back

My mother and father were saved at the age of 15 and 16 years. I was born on November 2, 1963. I was born in the church and I would see Saints back then taking time with the children of God. Sharing the love of God. And, let me tell you, it was real because you could feel the love and the presence of God all around them. When they would sing the song, "this joy that I have, the world didn't give it to me and the world can't take it away," I knew the word of God was true.

Some Saints might say they don't have the gift of evangelizing. I say anybody that God has shown love and that has been saved from their sins should be able to tell others that God can do the same for them. But, Saints, you have to pray and ask God to help you take that first step. Just tell God you are willing because He is already waiting for you. He's not going to force you. God is looking for people to obey Him and His word.

Loved one, when God puts assignments on your life, you can't hang around everybody because everybody is not going to receive the calling to go to the vineyard to reach His people. I believe getting away from some of those spirits that people are bringing; the vineyard mission will free you.

Matthew 28:19
___

Go ye therefore, and teach all nations, baptizing them in the name of the Father, and the Son, and of the Holy Ghost.

Just look how God calls twelve men to go out in the vineyard. And when God called them, He didn't just send them out in the vineyard without giving them power against unclean spirits, and power to heal all manner of sickness and all manner of disease. We are no different than those twelve disciples. God is telling us the same thing today, to go feel His sheep, and tell them the Kingdom of Heaven is at hand.

Matthew 10:38

And he that taketh not up his cross, and followeth after me, is not worthy of me.

Your souls will feel so good on the inside if you are brave and have no fear. God wants His people to rest in him. The vineyard needs real Saints that are going to love like Jesus loves. Therefore, let's slow down and let God do the work on the inside of our souls.

The most famous evangelist of our times, Billy Graham, presents the Gospel in a very straight forward manner, without manipulation or emotional trappings. Who could account for his success? The numbers of people who flock to Christ under his ministry? It is clear that the Holy Spirit was working though him.

Galatians 6:9

And let us not be weary in well doing: for in due season we shall reap, if we faint not.

Therefore, let us start pleasing God and not people. Saints are always saying they want to sow a seed. The best seed to sow is the word of God to the world. Just look at the prison system, where many of God's children are locked up because they didn't get to know about

Jesus. And maybe some did, but these people were not in the church when they did wrong. They were out in the vineyard. If we could only meet with them in the vineyard before they commit a crime and tell them about the Love of Jesus, they would made the right choice.

Saints, this earthly place is not our home, so let's not get caught up in the earth, but rather let's get caught up in the things that God wants us to do. Let His will be done in our lives.

John 10:10

The thief cometh not, but for to steal, and to kill, and to destroy: I am come that they might have life, and that might have it more abundantly.

I love, one of Martin Luther King Jr.'s speeches, when he said "Don't let no man pull you low enough to hate him." That's God speaking those words through him. Everything someone does to hurt you, God will let it work out for your good.

Once, for many nights, I cried, worried, feared, and has bad anxiety attacks. I didn't know that not forgiving someone for what they did to me was not only was affecting my health, but also my walk with God because, again, love is the key to open up the door to God. I took my problem to God and He put love where there was hate.

Mark 4:19

And the cares of the world, and deceitfulness of riches, and the lusts of other things entering in, and choke the word, and it becomes unfruitful.

Matthew 11:29

Take my yoke upon you, and ye learn of me; for I am meek and lowly in heart: and ye shall find rest unto your soul.

God is very good, so let us Saints cease to be spectators and start to be participants in the vineyard movement. There's so much work to be done. Jesus is still there waiting on the Saints to come walk with Him.

Look at Zachariah and what the Bible says he said when he heard about Jesus walking, and healing, saving souls and setting people free; he wanted to see Jesus. He did whatever it took to see Jesus. That's what the unbeliever will do if they hear about the Saints out on the highways and streets with the light of Jesus shining through them. You won't have to find sinners and unbelievers: they are going to be in front looking for you on every corner. They are looking for the love of God. Vineyard work is very important. People are hurting for Jesus because everything the church is looking for is in the vineyard. All the gifts of God are there. Preachers, Teachers, Gifts of Healing.

Pray for each other. Go out in the vineyard together because it's not about the pulpit—it is about the altar. The altar can be a sidewalk, a nightclub, the shopping center, the mall. It's everywhere. Can't you see the sign of the time?

Another great thing about the vineyard is that you won't have a program. You won't look at your watch to see if you have been in church too long. There, the Holy Ghost can have its way, without preventing you from going about your daily life. I know we have to make a living.

2 Thessalonians 3:10

For-ever when we were with you, this we commanded you, that if any would not work, neither let him eat.

The vineyard work will give us time to fellowship with one another. God will be getting us ready for heaven. He will want to know if we can love Him and praise Him together here on earth. People are dying out there, Saints. Let's go to the vineyard.

Love Them Enough to Pull Them out of the Fire

Acts 20:28

Take heed therefore unto yourselves, and to all the flock, over which the Holy Ghost hath made you overseers, to feed the church of God, which He has purchased with His own blood.

If we don't go out into the fields and feed God's sheep, how can they come to the house of God? They don't know it's ok to come as you are. They don't know that God loves them just the way they are.

God said the prayers of the righteous man availed much. Let us pray for one another. We all want to see Jesus when He returns for us. In praying, we might find healing and there is forgiveness of sin. That is why God said to pray without ceasing; we can't do anything without prayer.

We don't have to be afraid of anything as long as we seek God first. Because He has our back.

Chapter 5: The Love of God Will Always Be for the Vineyard

God doesn't want anyone to go to hell—Young or Old.

2 Chronicles 7:14

If my people will are called by my name, shall humble themselves, and pray, and seek my face, and turn from there wicked ways; then will I hear from heaven, and I will forgive their sin, and will heal their land.

Heaven is going to be a place where there will be no more dying, no more sickness, no more worrying. God wants every one of His children to be there. That's why He had His Son, named Jesus,to die for our sins.

Isaiah 64:6

But we are all as an unclean thing, and all our righteousness are as fitly rags; and we all do fade as a leaf; and our iniquities, like the wind have taken us away.

I hear people say all the time that the devil is busy. Well, so is the almighty God busy, too. Stop giving the devil praise; God deserves all the praises. God said we shall have dominion over the earth, not just so you can have a nice car, a big house. It's for Him. You were not born just to go to heaven—you must bring heaven down here to earth.

Matthew 6:24

No man can serve two masters: for he either he will hate the one, or love the other; or else he will hole to one, and despise the other. Ye cannot serve God and mammon.

And in the name of Jesus, I want to speak to you about the love of money.

1 Timothy 6:10

For the love of money is the root of all evil: which some coveted after, they have erred from the faith, and pierced themselves through with many sorrows.

That means if you are taking God's money and not sharing, and not showing love with the money He has blessed you with, then you are doing evil things with it. People think when they have money they have power. The only true power is the Holy Ghost Power. Let's back up, the number one thing in the world today is that people are not grateful to God our Lord Jesus Christ. We are taking God for granted.

It's not the economy. It's that people are not thankful to God. If we just take time to look around and see how good God is, then we won't have time to worry. And, lo and behold, the people who are complaining are Saints and people that have money! They are people who have food, and a place to lay their heads! Now tell me that not a blessing all by itself.

1 Timothy 6:8-9

---

[8]And having food and raiment let be there with content.

⁹But they that will be rich fall into temptation and a snare, and into many foolish and hurtful lusts, which down men in destruction and perdition.

God said we brought nothing into this world, and it is certain we can carry nothing out. I see around me people gathering up the wrong things: everything but the word of God. The way is not money, cars, and land. Being content and getting ready for the coming of Christ is the way.

I don't think lots of believers and truly feel that Jesus is coming back. Let me tell you that He is coming back quite soon. Now is the time God wants us to forget about these worldly things and put our love and our minds on Him. If you get connected to the true and living God, you won't need to worry about money or anything in this world. Money is just a tool to get the things we need in this world. The important thing, the thing which you need when Jesus comes, cannot be bought with money.

1 Timothy 6:11-12

¹¹But thou, man of God, flee these things; and follow after righteousness, godliness, faith, love, patience, meekness.

¹²Fight the good fight of faith, lay hold on eternal life, whereunto thou art also called, and hast professed a good profession before many witnesses.

Because most of the sickness is in the world today is because of worry about money.

Isaiah 55:1

Ho, every one that thirstieth, come ye to the water, and he that hath no money; come ye, buy, and eat: yea, come, buy wine and milk without money and without price.

God is telling us that if we walk upright by Him we won't have to worry about anything because the favor of God is worth it all. And God will provide. This is not our home, so if you have lost your home down here, don't worry about it, just move to another place. God said we have a home not made with hands.

Habakkuk 2:4

Behold, his soul which is lifted up is not upright in him: but the just shall live by faith.

Acts 8:20

But Peter said unto him, Thy money perish with thee, because thou hast thought that the gift of God may be purchase with money.

Peter is saying that what God has in store for His people, money can't buy.

Malachi 3:8-9

---

[8]Will a man rob God? Yet ye have robbed me. But ye say, where- in have we robbed thee? In tithes and offerings.
[9]Ye are cursed with a curse: for ye have robbed me, even this whole nation.

That is what causes money to worry people; they won't obey the word of God.

Malachi 4:10

Being ye all the tithes into the store- house, that there may be meat in my house, and prove me now here-with, saith the Lord of hosts, if I will not open you the windows of heaven, and pour you out a blessing that there shall not be room enough to receive it.

Whatever you give to God, He will give back to you. You won't always get your blessing in money. You can receive it though healing, loved ones saved. God has His own way of blessing us. The ones that are in need of a blessing, let us obey the word of the Lord. Not only will you be blessed, you will feel blessed also.

Only in being obedient to the word of God, and believing the word of God, can we be blessed.

Malachi 3:11

And I will rebuke the devourer for your sakes, and shall not destroy the fruits there of your ground; neither shall your vine cast her fruit before the time in the field, saith the Lord of host.

To serve Him you must obey all His commandments. What is wrong with our lives today? We are looking for restoration, but we don't want to obey. God can and will restore. If you are not ready to commit to God in His vineyard, stop looking for healing or a blessing.

Revelation 3:15 -17

[15]I know thy works, that thou art neither cold nor hot, I would thou wert cold or hot.

¹⁶So than because thou art lukewarm, and neither cold nor hot, I will spue thee out of thou mouth. ¹⁷Because thou sayest, I am rich, and increased with goods, and have need of nothing; and knowest not that thou art wretched, and miserable, and poor, and blind, and naked.

God has given power to us over all these unclean spirits. Did you hear what I just said? *Power*. The Holy Ghost's power. Paul in the book of Philippians asks them to pray; it's the only way you can get to Jesus.

Matthew 7:21

Not everyone that saith unto me Lord, Lord, shall enter into the kingdom of heaven; but he that doeth the will of my Father which is in heaven.

Every believer is justified before God to be an eternal 'heir to all that is God has made available. If we're just running, lying, even beating up the Saints, and robbing the Saints, and the church, trying to get all that God has promised us, but doing all these wrong and sinful things—you will not get into heaven. And you certainly won't get you the things God has promised you while you here on this earth. It's going to take Love.

Titus 1:2

In hope eternal life, which God, that cannot lie, promised before the world began.

We must believe. Christians should not speak evil of anyone. We should never let our speech be such that we could be condemned or bring disgrace to the ways of the Lord. Sin is a disgrace to God.

Titus 3:3

For we ourselves also were sometimes foolish, disobedient, deceived, serving divers lusts and pleasures ,living and malice and envy, hateful, and hating one another.

Titus 3:5

Not by works of righteousness which we have done, but according to His merry He saved us, by the washing of regeneration and renewing of the Holy Ghost.

I know that God is speaking to His children. He wants the best for all His children.

John 15:1-8

---

[1]I am the true vine, and my Father is the husbandman.
[2]Every branch in me that beareth not fruit He taketh away: and every branch that beareth fruit, He purgeth it, that it may bring forth more fruit.
[3]Now ye are clean through the word which I have spoken unto you.
[4]Abide in me, and I in you. As the branch cannot bear fruit of itself, excerpt it abide in the vine; no more can ye, excerpt ye abide in me.
[5]I am the vine, ye are the branches: He that abideth in me, and I in him, the same bringeth forth much fruit : for without me ye can do nothing.
[6]If a man abide not in me, he is cast forth as a branch, and is withered; and men gather them , and cast them into the fire, and they are burned.
[7]If ye abide in me, and my words abide in you, ye shall ask what ye will, and it shall be done unto you.
[8]Herein is my Father glorified, that ye bear much fruit; so shall ye be my disciples.

What is wrong with believers today, trying to fight in this war alone? We need Jesus, we need Jesus. I know you hear the name Jesus, but do you know him? Do you know that He and His Father are real? And that He's coming back soon?

We are going to have to die to ourselves, and get in the Spirit. That's the only way. That's when the miracle is going to take place in Jesus' name.

Colossians 3:1-3

---

¹If ye then be risen with Christ, seek those things which are above, where Christ sitteth on the right hand of God.
² Set your affection on things above, not on things on the earth.
³For ye are dead, and your life hid with Christ, in God.

God is telling us to put away all these things of the world, things such as not loving one another, gossiping, adultery, fornicating, lying, and everything else that is sinful. Then the things of this world will not matter to you. God wants us to think about our lives and the lives of others. Immorality, impurity, passion, evil desire, and greed, which amounts to idolatry, are the things that will bring the wrath of God upon the sons of disobedience. All we have to do is to put on love. It's the perfect bond of unity.

I want to speak to you about Love. Did you not know that the key to life in heaven is love? The way to get closer to God is love? I wish you, just for ten days, would ask God to help you love your neighbor, your children, your co-workers, your enemy, your husband, your wife, your fellow church member, and your preacher. Just surround yourself with love and watch God reveal himself to you in a mighty way. Healing will start taking place. Deliverance will start taking place. Everything you ever hoped for and desired will start taking place if you will simply love.

1 Peter 2:9

But ye are a chosen generation, a royal priesthood, an holy nation, a peculiar people: that ye should shew forth the praises of Him who hath called you out of darkness into His marvellous light.

God already knows the beginning to the end. Yes, it is full of unspeakable joy and Glory, but the other half has never been told.

The unbelievers just want to see us out there where they are. Most of them are backsliders who already have their mind on coming back to Jesus. We need to be like the father in the Prodigal son, one of the Jesus' parables. It appears in only one of the Canonical gospels of the New Testament. According the gospel of Luke (Luke 15:11-32), a father gives his two sons their inheritance before he dies. The inheritance allowed one of the sons to leave his father's house and go out in that world of sin, just like men do today, leaving God and doing anything they want to do. When you are not obeying the word of God, you have left your father. He will not stop you from leaving, but He still loves you.

After the son had spent everything, there was a severe famine in that whole country and he began to be in need. God allowed him to be hired out to a citizen of that country, who sent the son to his fields to feed pigs. He longed to fill his stomach with the pods that the pigs were eating but no one gave him anything. Then he came to his senses. He said that his father's servants were eating better than he was. So he went back to his father's house.

He was a long way off and his father saw him and was filled with compassion for him. The father threw his arms around his son and kissed him. But the son thought he was not worthy to be called the son. Still, the father put the best robe on him and had a celebration in honor of his return.

We have to let them know that no matter how many times we fall, we must get back up and ask God to forgive us from our sins. Don't just keep on sinning, because God won't tolerate that. Run to your Father who is in heaven. We must get forgiveness in every area of our life. Even working in the church as an usher, you must be born again and have the love of God in you! The definition of an usher is a person who helps ensure a smoothly running church service, and who ministers to the people in a variety of practical ways. Therefore, be careful when you take a position in the house of God because the vineyard is coming in to worship. And they're going to be looking for love of Jesus.

I could hear some of the older Saints singing the song *I'll go Lord. If I had to go by myself.* They were real, too. Sometimes when you are witnessing to someone, all it takes is a little bit of Jesus.

Romans 8:1

There is therefore now no condemnation to them who are in Christ Jesus, who walk not after the flesh, but after the Spirit.

Hosea 10:12

Sow to yourselves in righteousness, reap in mercy; break up your fallow ground: for it is time to seek the Lord, till he come and rain righteousness upon you.

Hebrews 4:12

For the word of God is quick and powerful, and sharper than any twoedged sword, piercing even to the dividing asunder of soul and spirit, and of the joints and marrow, and is a discerner of the thoughts and intents of heart.

He loves us. We don't have to fear.

James 4:7-8

---

⁷Submit yourself therefore to God. Resist the devil, and he will flee from you.
⁸Draw nigh to God, and He will draw nigh to you. Cleanse your hands, ye sinner: and purify your hearts, ye double minded.

Leviticus 19:17

Thou shalt not hate thy brother in thine heart: you shalt in any wise rebuke thy neighbor, and not suffer sin upon him.

Matthew 19:19

Honor thy father and thy mother: and, Thou shalt love thy neighbor as thyself.

And the way to love ourselves is to love God first, not the things of this world.

Mark 4:19

And the cares of this world, and the deceitfulness of riches, and the lusts of other things entering in, choke the word, and it becometh unfruitful.

All it takes is keeping our minds on things above. So many times, the word of God tells us that we are so blessed. We don't have to worry about anybody blessing us but God. He has the real blessing.

Genesis 12:3
___

And I will bless them that bless thee, and curse him that curse thee: and in thee shall all families of the earth be blessed.

Deuteronomy 4:31
___

(For the Lord thy God is merciful God;) He will not forsake thee, neither destroy thee, nor forget the covenant of thy fathers which He sware them.

Isaiah 1:19
___

If ye be willing and obedient, ye shall eat the good of the land.

1 Corinthians 2:9
___

But as it is written, Eye hath not seen, nor ears heard, neither have entered into the heart of man, the things which God hath prepared for them that love him.

All He wants His children to do is to love and obey.

Leviticus 11:44

For I am the Lord your God: ye shall therefore sanctify yourselves, and ye shall be holy; for I am holy: neither shall ye defile yourselves with any manner of creeping thing that creepeth upon the earth.

Peter 1:4

To an incorruptible, and undefiled, and that fadeth not away, reserved in heaven for you.

Revelation 2:26-29

---

[26]And he that overcometh, and keepeth my works unto the end, to him will I give power over the nations.
[27]And shall rule them with a rod of iron; as the vessels of a potter shall they be broken to shivers: ever as I received of my Father.
[28]And I will give him the morning star.
[29]He that hath an ear, let him hear what the Spirit saith unto the churches.

So if you don't have Love, just stop thinking you are going to heaven and stop working hard trying to get there. God is not talking about the kind of love you just speak about. He is talking about the kind of love you are to be about, to feel and to believe. If you don't have it, it's not too late. Just ask God to give you this love in your heart that Jesus has. He already knows you need it: He is just waiting on you to ask Him for it.

James 4:2

Ye lust, and have not: ye kill, and desire to have, and cannot obtain: ye fight and war, ye ask not, because ye ask not.

God is not a God who will force His love on anyone; He could because He is God. But He is so good and loving He gives us a choice in this world because this world was built on Love.

John 3:16

For God so loved the world, that He gave His only begotten Son, that whosoever believeth in Him should not perish, but have everlasting life.

God loves us: He is asking for Love. And His word is true because it is the word is God.

Revelation 3:5

He that overcometh, the same shall be clothed in white raiment; and I will not blot out his name out of the book of life, but I will confess his name before my Father, and before His angels.

God is telling us again.

Revelation 3:13

He that hath an ear, let him hear what the Spirit saith unto the churches.

1 John 1:9

If we confess our sins, He is faithful and just to forgive us our sins, and to cleanse us from all unrighteousness."

All it takes is to have a little talk with Jesus.

James 5:16

Confess your faults one to another, and pray one for another, that ye may be healed. The effectual fervent prayer of a righteous man availeth much.

Paul is telling us.

Galatians 2:20

I am crucified with Christ: nevertheless I live; yet not I, but Christ liveth in me: and the life which I now live in the flesh. I live by the faith of the Son of God, who Lord me, and gave himself for **me**.

If we only knew how mush God really loves us. We say that God loves me, but do you believe He loves you?

Matthew 17:20

And Jesus said unto them, Because of your unbelief: for verily I say unto you, If ye have faith as a grain of mustard seed, ye shall say this mountain, remove hence to yonder place. and it shall remove: and nothing shall be impossible unto you.

Dearly beloved, you can hardly see a mustard seed. All it takes is a little bit of faith: The effectual fervent prayer of a righteous man availed much. So too can we plead the blood over one another in the name of Jesus.

I pray that we all be ready when Jesus comes. This deadly thing called sin is something that every man comes into this world with. But the greatest thing is that Jesus died for our sins so that we might be saved.

Sin is the only thing can separate us from God.

Isaiah 30:1
___

Woe to the rebellious children, saith the Lord, that counsel, but not of me; and that cover with a covering, but not of my spirit, that they may add sin to sin.

We are a blessed people because if it weren't for Jesus going to the cross and dying for our sins, He wouldn't have power over the enemy. That's why, living free from sin, we can live again after death with Jesus Christ. Being saved from sin takes a daily walk with Christ because every day we have to fight the good fight of faith to live free from sin.

1 Corinthians 15:34
___

Awake to righteousness, and sin not; for some have not the knowledge of God: I speak to your shame.

Just think, before we were born

Romans 5:12-13
___

[12]Wherefore, as by one man sin entered into the world, and death by sin; and so death passed upon all

men, for that all have sinned.
[13]For until the law sin was in the world: but sin is not imputed when there is no law.

That's why by one man, Jesus Christ, being obedient to His Father, many shall be made righteous.

Roman 6: 12
___

Let not sin therefore reign in your mortal body, that ye should obey it in the lusts thereof.

Romans 6:14-15
___

[14]For sin shall not have dominion over you, for ye are not under law but under grace.
[15]What then? shall we sin, because we are not under the law, but under grace? God forbid.

When we come into Christ and ask Him to come into our lives and save us from our sins.

Romans 6:6
___

Knowing this, that our old man is crucified with him, that the body of sin might be destroyed, that hence forth we should not serve sin.

Romans 6:23

For the wages of sin is death; but the gift of God is eternal life through Jesus Christ our Lord.

We must live a holy life before God. There is no other way. Because if you are the richest person in this world, and you don't have Jesus in your life, you are living in sin, you are a slew.

Not having faith in God is a sin.

Romans 14:23

And he that doubteth is damned if he eat, because he eateth not of faith: for whatsoever is not of faith is a sin.

So we must walk in the fear of God and obey His word, so He can keep us from sinning, every hour, minute, and every second. We know not when the Lord Jesus is coming back.

1 Thessalonians 5:2

For yourselves know perfectly that the day of the Lord so cometh as a thief in the night.

We must be ready. That's why God said to pray without ceasing. Saints of God and People of God, prayer is the only way to see Jesus face.

I love that song that Hezekiah Walker sang:

> I need you. You need me.
> We all are God's body.
> Stand with me. Agree with me.
> We all are God's body.
> It is His will that every need be supplied.
> You are important to me: I need you to survive.

How we can sing the song when we all get to heaven. What a day of rejoicing that will be. And we can't rejoice with each other hear on earth.

Psalm 139:14

I will praise thee; for I am fearfully and wonderfully made: marvelous are thy works; and that my soul knoweth right well.

Chapter 6: A Question

I want to ask you a question. Have you ever had something terrible happen in your life that you couldn't handle? I want to answer that question: yes, I have. And nobody could handle it but God. I tried to fight, but I realized that God is the only one who could help me. We are letting the world take over. And Saints are doing nothing about it. Look at David.

1 Samuel 17:37

David said moreover, The Lord that delivered me out the paw of the lion, and out of the paw of the bear, and He will deliver me out of the hand of this Philistine. And Saul said unto David go, and the Lord be with thee.

Samuel 17:45

Then said David to the Philistine, Thou comest to me with a sword, and with a spear, and with a shield: but

I come to thee in the name of the Lord of host, the God of the armies of Israel, whom thou hast defiled.

In my life time, I have attended funerals and I have seen people loving, caring for the one that God has called home. But by then it's too late to show that kind of love and kindness, so let's do it now, while we still have time. We must go out and do the work of God. It's time to obey. Some don't believe the word of God is real. Some unbelievers don't believe. But it's real, so real.

Deuteronomy 7:9

Know therefore that the Lord thy God, he is God the faithful God, which keepth covenant and mercy with them that love Him and keep His commandments to a thousand generations.

Matthew 24:46-51

[46]Blessed is that servant, whom the Lord when He cometh shall find so doing's.
[47]Verily I say unto you, That He shall make him ruler over all the goods.
[48]But and if that evil servant shall say in his heart, My Lord delayeth, His coming;
[49]And shall begin to smite his fellow servant, and to eat and drink with the drunken;

⁵⁰The Lord of that servant shall come in a day when he looketh not for him, and in an hour that he is not aware of,
⁵¹And shall cut him asunder, and appoint him his portion with the hypocrites: there shall be weeping and gnashing of teeth.

So you can stay in the Spirit, and so you can hear from God and be a true disciple of God. There are all kinds of spiritual gifts, but the first gift is the gift of love for God and His vineyard.

1 Corinthians 12:1-11

¹Now concerning spiritual gifts, brethren, I would not have you ignorant.
²Ye know that ye were Gentiles, carried away unto there dumb idols, ever as ye were led.
³Wherefore I give you to understand, that no man speaking by the Spirit of God calleth Jesus accursed: and that no man can say that Jesus is the Lord, but by the Holy Ghost.
⁴Now there are diversities of gifts, but the same Spirit.
⁵And there are differences of administrations, but the same Lord.
⁶And there are diversities of operation, but it is the same God which worketh all in all.
⁷But the manifestation of the Spirits is given to profit withal.

> [8] For to one is given by the Spirit the word of wisdom; to another the word of knowledge by the same Spirit;
> [9] To another faith by the same spirit; to another the gifts of healing by the same spirit;
> [10] To another the working of miracles: another prophecy: to another discerning of spirits: to another the interpretation of tongues:
> [11] But all these worketh that one and the selfsame spirit, dividing to every man severally as he will.

What the Bible is telling us is that you must be in the Spirit to do any of His work.

It's time, Saints, to put God first. Because there is nothing you cannot do without God. When David went in the name of God, the fight was over, and he won. That's the only way, Saints. When we pray and seek God every day, every hour and every minute, this nation will change. And, if this nation will put God back into everything they took Him out of, all this killing, all this hate, all this sickness, all this hunger for money will stop. God is waiting. For whoever took Him out to put Him back.

What if all the churches were like David? And let the Lord have His way, and put Him first in everything. The vineyard will be full of Saints sold out for Jesus.

Saints, "Satan hasn't forgotten about us; he designs your capture and re-enslavement." The evil army is seeking ways to 'rob us of happiness, steal our future, and to destroy us.

John 10:10

The thief cometh not, but for to steal and to kill, and to destroy: I am come that they might have life and that they might have it more abundantly.

Yes, we are saved and have the Lord on our side. But it is still "a jungle out there "and the "roaring lion" is still on the prowl!

1 Peter 5:8-9

[8]Be sober, be vigilant: because your adversary the devil, as a roaring lion, walketh about, seeking whom he may devour: [9]Whom resist steadfast in the faith, knowing afflictions are accomplished in your brethren that are in the world.

God loves us so much. We most get together in one accord before Jesus comes back. The book of Titus, Paul tells us, that *"Christians are exhorted not only to live pure lives, but to have pure motives as well."*

Yes, we are all of one body in Christ. When we go out in the vineyard to work heartily, as for the Lord, asking God to give us wisdom and tell us how.

Philippians 2:1-8

---

[1]If there be therefore consolation in Christ, if any comfort of love, if any fellowship of the Spirit, if any bowels and mercies,

[2]Fulfill ye my joy, that ye be like minded, having the same love, being of one accord, of one mind.

[3]Let nothing be done through strife or vainglory; but in lowliness of mind let each esteem other better then themselves.

[4]Look not every man on his own things, but every man also on the things of other.

[5]Let this mind be in you, which was also in Christ Jesus:

[6]Who, being in the form of God, thought is not robbery to be equal with God:

[7]But made himself of no reputation, and took upon Him the form a servant, and was made in the likeness of men:

[8]And being found in fashion as a man, He humbled himself, and became obedient unto death, even the death of the cross.

It's all up to the believers to start truly believing God's word.

Philippians 4:13

I can do all things through Christ which strengthened me.

God said He will never leave us or forsake us. I know we have members in our churches who don't engage in fellowship with other churches. That's where the body of Christ is failing and losing their blessings, their healing, their children, their marriages; everything that God desires His people to have, they are losing. It's because they won't get together to fast and pray and love and seek His face. Just think, if all the believers get together of one accord, then the enemy wouldn't have a change to mess with God's people. Real Saints must get together and pray for one another.

And God cares. But God wants me to let you know today that life and time on this earth is short. We have no time to waste, and the enemy is doing and using everything we can to take God's people with him. God is good! Yes He is. But if we don't stop and obey Gods word, we can't go back with him.

Matthew 5:8

Blessed are the pure in heart, for they shall see God.

Whatever God's word says is true! Saints, this earthly place is not our home, so let's get caught up in the things that God wants us to do. And let His will be done in our life.

Some Saints might say they don't have the gift of evangelizing; I say anybody to whom God has shown love and has saved from their sins should be able to tell others that God can do the same for them. You have to pray and ask God to help you take that first step; just tell God you are willing because He is already waiting for you. He's not going to force it on you. God is looking for people to obey Him and His word.

Matthew 28:19

Go ye therefore, and teach all nations, baptizing them in the name of the Father, and the Son, and of the Holy Ghost.

Romans 1:16

For I am not ashamed of the gospel, Of Christ: for it is the power of God unto salvation to every -one that believeth; of the Jew first, and also the Greek.

Luke 21:1-3

[1]And He looked up, and saw the rich men casting their gifts into the treasury.

²And He saw also a certain poor widow casting in thither two mites. ³And He said, Of a truth I say unto you, that this poor widow hath cast in more than they all:

So I say this; you don't have to be rich to tell someone about Jesus.

Psalm 50:10

For every beast of the forest is mine, and the cattle upon a thousand hills.

We have sheep going astray in the vineyard; Bishop and pastor are sitting around waiting on the program, and for members to go out on one Saturday of the mouth. That should not be so. Every day a group of Saints, and every church that God is the head of, all over this world, are in the street feed up with laboring for God; the time is near. This is not about program; this is about the souls that need to know about Jesus Christ. The Bible says "if ye suffer for righteousness sake happy are ye." Let us be suffering for God sake. All we have to do to evangelize is be ready at all times to tell someone about the hope that is within you and that God will being that same hope to every man. All the Saints must get together, all over this world, and act hospitably toward one to another without grudging.

65

1 Peter 5:10

But the God of all grace, who hath called us unto His eternal glory by Christ Jesus, after that ye have suffered a while make you perfect, stablish strengthen, settle you.

God has delayed His coming soon that more may come to repentance. And righteousness shall prevail over wickedness in the end. Destruction comes to those who scoff at the word of God. We must be obedient to the word of God. God is not looking for the traditional believer; He is looking for the righteous believer, one who is going to stand. A lot of people in the vineyard already know about Jesus, but do they know the truth about Jesus? That He is coming back soon and He wants to set them free? That which the Son set free is free indeed? The Saints are the pictures of God to the world, so if you are not walking like God, the unbeliever will know.

We need a Street Revival. What is a revival? A revival is "an awakening, in a church or community, of interest in and care for matters relating to personal religion. An improvement, recovery, rallying, picking up, turn for the better, upturn, upswing, resurgence." This is what the vineyard needs. There is nothing wrong with sharing the word of God, on Face book, Internet, or texting on the phone. But is that what Jesus did? No matter how much we do or say on this new world system, that's still not what Jesus did. Don't get me wrong—keep witnessing, but that is the world's way. The only way is Jesus. He wanted to show love and His power, and for you to be about His Father's business.

The Lord didn't just ask that we help Him in sharing the word of God with others; He commands it. Look at Moses. He didn't want to do it, but God convinced him to take the calling.

I want to tell the young people, "God is calling you out in the vineyard to do the work of the Lord. There is plenty of work for you to do. So don't be afraid."

Psalm 34:4

I sought the Lord, and He answered me: and delivered me from all my fears.

Come on, young people, let's get out to do the work of the Lord.

1 Timothy 4:12

Do not let anyone look down on you because you are young, but set an example for the believers in speech, in conduct, in love, and faith, and in purity.

God doesn't want anyone to go to hell Young or old. God said in

Philippians 2:10

That at the name of Jesus every knee should bow, of things in heaven and here on earth, and things in the earth; and things under the earth

The vineyard must know. By going to the street your labor won't be in vain.

Corinthians 15:58

Therefore, my beloved brethren, be ye steadfast, unmovable, always abounding in the work of the Lord, forasmuch as ye know that your labour is not and vain in the Lord.

God will bless you! It's not about pleasing men; it's about pleasing God.

Galatians 1:10

For do I now persuade men, or God? or do I seek to please men? for if I yet pleased men I should not be the servant of Christ.

God has enough people in the churches to have the streets full every minute of the day.

Jeremiah 18:1-2

---

¹The word of which came to Jeremiah from the Lord, saying,
²Arise, and go down to the potter's house, and there I will cause thee to hear my words.

Jeremiah obeyed God. That's what it's all about: God's word. He knew the vessel couldn't fix itself. We as children of God must stop trying to fix ourselves and let God do it. Because we all have a sinful nature, and every time we disobey God, fixing ourselves gets harder and harder.

The world is looking for Jesus. There is so much work to be done. When Jesus was walking on this earth He was out in the vineyard, and He is still there waiting on the Saints to come walk with Him. I don't know about you, but it's a great feeling to let someone know that God loves them and He can save them from their sins.

All God wants are Holy mens because He can use you. There are souls needing to know Jesus. We say all the time we love the Lord.

John 21:15

So when they had dined, Jesus saith to Simon Peter, Simon, son of Jonas, lovest thou me more than these? He saith unto him, Yea Lord; thou knowest that I love thee. He saith to him, feed my lambs.

He is asking the Saints the same question.

John 21:6

And Jesus said unto them, Cast the net on the right side of the ship, and ye shall find. They cast therefore, and now they were not able to draw it for the multitude of fishes.

God is telling the church the same thing—to go into the vineyard. He will be there all the way. Trust Him with whatever you have to give for the Gospel and get up and get out and fish for men. Supernatural blessings will fall upon your life.

He told Peter from now on He will make you fishers of men. You must believe God.

2 Timothy 4:1-5

---

[1]I charge thee therefore before God, and the Lord Jesus Christ, who shall judge the quick and the dead at His appearing and His kingdom;
[2]Preach the word; be instant in season, out of season; reprove, rebuke, exhort with all long suffering and doctrine.
[3]For the time will come when they will not endure sound doctrine; but after their own lusts shall they harp to themselves teachers, having itching ears;
[4]And they shall turn away their ears from the truth, and shall be turned unto fables.
[5]But watch thou in all things, endure afflictions, do the work of an evangelist, make full proof of thy ministry.

We have a lot of false prophets running around here today. The unbelievers know them. I challenge you every Saint every believer to start getting a group of people to go out and the vineyard every day. You can go out by twos. You don't need a whole lot of people or a big group. If you and your sister in Christ can go out to the Mall and shop for two to three hours, you and your sister can go to the vineyard for two to three hours.

Come on, Saints, let's stop talking about the things that are going on in these last days and start getting the love of God to His people. Prayer is needed. Love is needed. Ask God to take away all yours fears so you can and do the work of the Lord. God will not ask us to do something without also giving us the provisions to do it well. It is impossible to live successful Christian lives apart from the Holy Spirit. Christians obedient to God's leading will have tremendous opportunities to share Christ with the world.

Saints all over the world, we must stay on one accord until Jesus comes.

Acts 8:4

Therefore they that were scattered abroad went everywhere preaching the word.

Acts 8:6

And the people with one accord gave heed unto those things which Philip spake, hearing and seeing the miracles which he did.

Again I tell you that the miracles are taking place in the vineyard.

Acts 8:8

And there was great joy in that city.

All of our cities and countries are waiting for that joy and that is to know about Jesus. Acts 13 tells us that the Holy Spirit calls Saul and Barnabas.

Acts 13:2-3

---

[2]As they ministered to the Lord, and fasted, the Holy Ghost said Separate me Barnabas and Saul for the work where unto I have called them.
[3]And when they had fasted and prayed, and laid their hands onthem, they sent them away.

This whole world needs to fast together and pray together so the Holy Ghost can send us into the vineyard to work. Paul had three missionary journeys because he knew that God's word is true. God's word is the fuel for a consistent lifestyle. Just like God sent Nehemiah to Jerusalem to help his people restore their city from the outside in, the Israelites not only rebuilt the walls and the city, but their lives as well. People are waiting to hear the word of God in the vineyard. Responding to God's word is the one of the greatest pathways to spiritual renewal. God's word will hold us accountable and will show us the way back. God's word is the only thing that can give us the proper spiritual direction we need in life. Walking with Christ brings us together in unity and purpose.

Acts 4:31

And when they had prayed, the place where they were assembled was shaken, and they were all filled with the Holy Ghost and thou to spake the word of God with boldness.

See, Saints, that's the way God wants us to be: loving one another, and helping when one is in need, no matter what it takes. The Bible tells us to love and care for one another. If we obey God's word we can have a touch of heaven right here on earth.

Psalm 133:1-3

¹Behold, how good and how pleasant it is for brethren to dwell together in unity!
²It is like the precious ointment upon the head, that ran down upon the beard ever Aaron's beard: that went down to the skirts of his garments:
³As the dew of Hermon, and as the dew that descended upon the mountains of Zion: for there the Lord command the blessing even life for evermore.

Again there are blessings in unity. We must put all our trust in the Lord's hand, trusting that God will fight for us. We must stop trying to fight the spiritual war without God.

Proverbs 3:5-7

---

⁵Trust in the Lord with all thine heart; and lean not unto thine own understanding.
⁶In all thy ways acknowledge him, and He shall direct thy paths.
⁷Be not wise in thine own eyes: fear the Lord, and depart from evil.

God is a good God because He tells us that He will bless us if we obey him.

Psalms 1:1-5

---

¹Blessed is the man that walketh not in the counsel of the ungodly, nor standed in the way of sinner's, nor sitteth in the seat of the scornful.
²But his delight is in the law of the LORD; and in His law doth he meditate day and night.
³And he shall be like a tree planted by the rivers of water, that bringeth forth his fruit in the season; his leaf also shall not wither and whatso ever he doeth shall proper.
⁴The ungodly are not so: but are like the chaff which the wind driveth away.
⁵Therefore the ungodly shall not stand in the judgment, nor sinners in the congregation of the righteous:

I pray that God keep you save from sin. I want to know as does the world need to know that one day death is coming. That death is the last thing that will be defeated.

Hosea 13:14

I will ransom them from the power of the grave; I will redeem them from death; O death, I will be thy plagues; O grave, I will be thy destruction: repentance shall be hid from mind eyes.

But when we die, it's not over yet. We have to get to the other side.

Matthew 16:28

Verily I say unto you, There be some standing here, which shall not taste of death, till they see the Son of man coming in His kingdom.

That's why we must live this life free from sin, no matter if we are in the grave or walking on this earth when Jesus comes back.

Philippians 2:8

And being found in fashion as a man, He humbled himself, and became obedient unto death, even the death of the cross.

Jesus died for you and for me, so because He had to die, so too are we going to leave this old body one day. However, if we are obedient to the word of God, like Jesus did, we won't have to worry about dying because there will be life after death.

Matthew 16:26
___

For what is a man profited, if he shall gain the whole world and lose his own soul? Or what shall a man give in exchange for his soul?

If His word is true; we brought nothing into this world, so why do we worry about the things that concern this world?

John 5:24
___

Verily, Verily, I say unto you, He that heareth my word, and believeth on Him that sent me, hath everlasting life, and shall not come into condemnation but is passed from death to life.

1 John 5:16
___

If any man see his brother sin a sin which is not unto death, he shall ask, and he shall give him life for them that sin not unto death, There is a sin unto death: I do not say that he shall pray for it.

Paul is telling us that we have to die daily. This means taking everything to God daily, and focusing on one day at the time, and not worry about tomorrow, because it's not promise to us.

1 Corinthians 15:55-56

[55]O death, where is thy sting? O grave, where is thy victory?
[56]The sting of death is sin: and the strength of sin is the law.

There is a natural body and there is a spiritual body. Paul tells us we have to submit to our Spiritual body.

1 Corinthians 15:58

Therefore my beloved brethren, be ye stedfast, unmovable, always abounding in the work of the Lord, for-as-much as ye know that your labour is not in vain in the Lord.

Revelation 1:18

I am He that liveth, and was dead; and, behold, I am alive for evermore; Amen; and have the keys of hell and of death.

Deuteronomy 30:15

See, I have set before thee this day life and good, and death and evil.

Isaiah 25:8

That He will swallow up death in victory; and the Lord God will wipe away tears from off all faces; and the rebuke of His people shall He take away from off all the earth: for the Lord hath spoken it.

I want to go back with Jesus when He comes back for His children. That's why I have to take it one day at the time.

John 3:30

He must increase, but I must decrease.

The old man has to die, Saints.

1 Peter 3:18

For Christ also hath once suffered for sins, the just for the unjust, that He might bring us to God, being put to death in the flesh, but quickened by the Spirit.

That is why it is so important that we have made Christ our Lord. If you don't know Him, please get to know Him so you can live again. People of Christ, don't let Christ come with our work undone; if you need Him just ask Him to deliver you from death to life.

You don't have to ask. He said that we know because righteousness shall prevail over the wickedness in the end. God wants all Saints to grow in grace and the knowledge of our Lord and Savior Jesus Christ. Christ wants us to have fellowship with one another, to love one another. The first fellowship is with God; we must talk and walk in obedience and the truth. This love is that Christ died for all, and He lay down His life for our sins, and we must let the vineyard know about that love. God is life. God is light. God is love.

This poor vineyard is waiting on you to be the hands and feet, to spread the Gospel of Jesus Christ before the end come. Just like in the day of Noah before the flood, people were doing as the believer and unbeliever are doing now. Drinking, marrying, and giving in marriage, not loving one another, not sharing the teachings of God, but instead being disobedient to the word of God. The Bible is fulfilling today: earthquakes, wars and rumors of wars.

Matthew 24:2

And Jesus said unto them, See ye not all these things? Verily I say unto you, These shall not be left here one stone upon another, that shall not be thrown down.

Matthew 24:51

And shall cut him asunder, and appoint him his portion with the hypocrites; there shall be weeping and gnashing of teeth.

Our God doesn't want us to go to Hell where there is nothing but torment for eternity.

Matthew 24:6

And ye shall hear of wars and rumours of wars: see that ye be not troubled: for all these things must come to pass, but the end is not yet.

Matthew 24:14

And this gospel of the kingdom shall be preached in all the world for a witness unto all nations: and then shall the end come.

Matthew 24:36

But of that day and hour knoweth no man, no, not the angels of heaven, but my Father only.

Matthew 24:44

Therefore be ye also ready: for in such an hour as ye think not the Son of man cometh.

The ones that will be doing and obeying His word when the Lord cometh will be blessed. This song the older Saints used to sing:

Love lifted me, Love lifted me,
When nothing else could help
Love lifted me.

That is true. Love is the only way. We say we have faith but faith works by love.

John 5:30

I can of mine own self do nothing: as I hear, I judge: and my judgment is just; because I seek not my own will, but the will of the Father which hath sent me.

That will was to love and die for you and me. And faith knows how to love.

Matthew 24:13

But he that shall endure unto the end, the same shall be saved.

God is talking about all of His children. Saints, if we want to hear from God, we are going to have to go outside these walls. Your life of faith will require living like God. We are not called to adopt the Bible to our culture but to adopt our culture to our Bible. Saints, This world is passing away: don't hang on to this world. There is hope— we have to follow hope, that hope of Jesus. He is waiting for you to work your faith.

We get hung up on time—we don't have time to reach out in the vineyard. You can have spiritual time and time of the flesh. The spiritual time is the only time that matters. God is always on time. In the fullness of time God sent His Son Jesus Christ. There is a time when God is coming back for His elected ones. Just like Ezekiel and the valley of dry bones. The Lord God told him to command the bones to live, to prophesy upon the dry bones, and to say unto them the word of the Lord, speaking life to them. This is the same way

God wants us to speak to His people that are dried up and bony without the Spirit so they can live externally with the Lord.

Isaiah 61:1

The Spirit of the Lord is upon me: because the Lord has anointed me to preach good tidings into the meek; He hath sent me to bind up the broken hearted, to proclaim liberty to the captives, and the opening of the prison to them that are bond; this is the acceptable year of the Lord.

My heart longs to serve God's people and the vineyard. The Lord is saying "he that as an ear let him hear" what the Spirit of the Lord is saying to the church about the vineyard.

Thank God for TBN for sharing all day long the word of God with the world. It's a blessing. My soul has been blessed. But there needs to be Saints out there in the fields sharing the gospel, too. Look at Jesus. He didn't have internet, megaphones, radios, TV. He walked in the fields, working miracles, saving people souls, healing, feeding the thousands. And we say we want to be like Jesus.

God is looking down on this whole world, waiting on us to grab hold of the key of love. We have to seek God with all our heart, so He can do His will for our lives.

Chapter 7: Love

The Revelation of the End is near. "This book is so named because it is the 'revelation of Jesus Christ as given to the Apostle John'. It is also called the 'Apocalypse', which means 'revelation' or 'unveiling'.

> "John is exiled by the Roman government to Patmos, a small island world of persecution off the coast of Greece, for preaching the word of God. His exile is only part of an intense period of persecution against the church which follows the Roman emperor Domitian's proclamation that he should be worshiped as deity."
>
> (Holman Rainbow Study Bible)

While he is on Patmos, John receives this revelation about Jesus Christ from God the Father. An angel helps John to understand the vision. Whereas the first book of the Bible, Genesis, tells of the beginning of sin and Satan's triumph, the last book of the Bible, Revelation, tells of God's triumph over all evil and His judgement of the wicked.

"A special blessing is promised to all who read and hear and obey this book. But also a special curse is promised to those who add to or take away from these words. John also wrote the fourth Gospel and three epistles which bear his name.

Revelation is lavish in colorful disclosure of the prophetic events which await every person, whether dead or alive. The Revelation lets us know what is to come: the series of devastations to be poured out upon the earth, the Mark of the Beast—666— the climactic battle of Armageddon, the blinding of Satan, the reign of the Lord, the great white throne of judgment and the nature of the eternal city of God.

Prophecies concerning Jesus Christ are fulfilled, and a concluding call to his Lordship assures us that He will soon return. Revelation, Jesus Christ, Seven—the book is a thorough "revelation" of the total person of Jesus Christ, His glory, power and wisdom; His judgment, kingdom and grace; and the Lamb of God from Alpha to Omega.

The number "seven" is dominate throughout with 7 Letters, 7 Seals, 7 Trumpets, 7 Signs, 7 Plagues, 7 Dooms, 7 New Things.

The end of earthy life is only the beginning of eternal life. Christians shall spend eternity with God in the New Jerusalem. Unbelievers shall spend eternal life with Satan in the lake of fire. God desires that everyone trust in His Son for redemption today."

(Holman Rainbow Study Bible)

My prayer is that every preacher start preaching in the Book of Revelation because it is so near and the unbeliever will know that there is life after death, that it does matter where they are going to spend eternity: Heaven or Hell. God is letting us know no matter what is taking place on this earth today that He is God almighty, the Alpha and the Omega: the beginning and the end.

The ones who hear the word and obey the word are going to be blessed with the greatest blessing ever—to spend eternity with God. He is coming with clouds and every eye shall see him and the ones who certified him. God is asking us in His word that if you are hanging on to anything that will keep you out of heaven turn it loose. Let it go. Fight to let it go. Be mindful and know that God is a Holy God and a loving God.

Revelation 1:14-15

---

[14]His head and His hairs were white like wool, as white as snow; and His eyes were as a flame of fire;

¹⁵And His feet like unto fine brass, as if they burned in a furnace; and His voice as the sound of many waters.

I don't know about you, but I want to go back with Jesus when He returns. You would have to have heavenly eyes just to see Him because an earthly eye won't be able to look at him. Read about the Apocalypse in the Bible and see what John said when he saw the Lord Jesus Christ.

Revelation 1:17-18

¹⁷And when I saw him, I fell at His feet as dead. And He laid His right hand upon me, saying unto me, Fear not: I am the first and the last:
¹⁸I am He that liveth, and was dead: and, behold, I am alive forevermore, Amen; and have the keys of hell and death.

God is speaking to the churches today to repent.

Revelation 2:7

He that hath an ear, let him hear what the spirit saith unto the churches: to him that overcometh will I give to eat of the tree of life, which is in the midst of the paradise of God.

God said that we are going to have tribulation but be faithful unto death, and He will give us the crown of Life.

Chapter 8: The Seven Letters of Revelation

(Letter 1)

Revelation 2:1-2

¹Unto the angel of the church of Ephesus write; These things saith He that holdeth the seven stars in His right hand, who walketh in the midst of the seven golden candlesticks;
²I know thy works, and thou labour and thy patience, and how thou canst not bear them which are evil: and thou tried them which say they are apostles, and are not, and hast found them liars:

Revelation 2:5

Remember therefore from whence thou are fallen, and repent, and do the first work: or else I will come unto thee quickly, and will remove thy candle stick out of His place, except thou repent.

(Letter 2)

Revelation 2:8-9

[8]And unto the angel of the church in Smyrna write; These things saith the first and the last, which was dead, and is alive;
[9]I know thy works, and tribulation, and poverty,(but thou art rich) and I know the blasphemy of them which say they are Jews, and are not but are the synagogue, of Satan. (Repent, God said, the ones that say they are holy Christian and are not.)

(Letter 3)

Revelation 2:12-13

[12]And to the angel of the church in Pergamos write; These things saith He which hath the sharp sword with two edges;
[13]I know thy works and where thou dwellest, even where Satan's seat is: and thou holdest fast my name, and hast not denied my faith, even in those

days wherein Antipas was my faithful martyr, who was slain among you, where Satan dwelleth."

(Letter 4)

Revelation 2:18-19

---

[18]And unto the angel of the church in Thyatira write; These things saith the Son of God, who hath His eyes like unto a flame of fire, and His feet are like fine brass;
[19]I know thy works and charity and service, and faith, and thy patience,and thy works; and the last to be more than the first.

God told them to repent from committing fornication.

Revelation 2:23

And I will kill her children with death; and all the churches shall know that I am He which searcheth the reins and hearts: and I will give unto every one of you according to your works.

Revelation 2:26

And he that overcometh, and keepeth my works unto the end, to him will I give power over the nations.

(Letter 5)

Revelation 3:1

And unto the angle of the church in Sandis write; These things saith He that hath the seven Spirits of God, and the seven stars; I know thy works, that thou hast a name that thou livest, and art dead.

Revelation 3:2

Be watchful, and strengthen the things which remain that are really to die: for I have not found thy works perfect before God.

God is saying to the Saints that think they done made it in already, and they are prefect to be watchful, because he will come as a thief, and the night. And will not know the hour thy will come upon thee. If you hold fast, you will walk with a white garment; your name will not be blot out the book of life.

(Letter 6)

Revelation 3:7-8

⁷And to the angel of the church in Philadelphia write;
These things saith He that is holy, He that is true, He
that hath the key of David, He that openeth, and no
man shutteth; and shutteth, and no man openeth;
⁸I know thy works: behold, I have set before thee an
open door, and no man can shut it: for thou hast litter
strength, and hast kept my word, and hast not denied
my name.

God tells the Saints that have kept His word to hold on and walk up
right with Him and that He loves them.

Revelation 3:12

Him that overcometh will I make a pillar in the temple
of God, and He shall go no more out: and I will write
upon him the name of my God, and the name of the
city of my God, which is new Jerusalem which
cometh down out of heaven from my God: and I will
write upon him my new name.

(Letter 7)

Revelation 3:14-16

---

[14]And unto the angel of the church of the Laodiceans write; These things saith the Amen, the faithful and true witness, the beginning of the creation of God; [15]I know thy works, that thou art neither cold nor hot: I would thou were cold or hot. [16]So then because thou art luke warm, and neither cold nor hot, I will spue thee out of my mouth.

Revelation 3:19

As many as I love, I rebuke and chasten: be zealous therefore, and repent.

God is saying that He loves us and that is why He rebukes and chastens us. Therefore, repent.

Revelation 3:20

Behold, I stand at the door, and knock: If any men hear my voice, and open the door, I will come in to him,and sup with him, and He with me.

Revelation 3:22

He that hath an ear, let him hear what the Spirit saith unto the churches.

"The throne of God is heaven." God is worthy of all our praise. He is sitting on the throne looking down on us and still loving and blessing us. Because He is Holy, Holy, Holy and He is Lord God Almighty. Repent so your name is written in the Lamb's book of life, the book that no man is worthy to open and loose the seal.

God is waiting and He is giving us time to repent before His throne. So, to wear that white robe you have to be wash in the blood of Jesus. He is the only one who can wash you white as snow.

Revelation 7:14

And I said unto him, Sir, thou knowest. and He said to me, these are they which come out of great tribulation, and have washed their robes, and made white in the blood of the Lamb.

Worthy is the Lamb and the ones who don't have the seal of God in their hearts and whose souls will be tormented in the pits of Hell. In the last days to come, men and women are going to want to die, but death shall flee from them. God is trying to warn us before that time about the end time and what going to happen if we are not connected to the Lamb. That we are overcome by the blood of the Lamb and the words of our testimony.

And we must know that we know the Lord because in the last days miracles will try to deceive the Saints.

Revelation 13:14

And deceiveth them that dwell on earth by the means of those miracles which had power to do in sight of the beast; saying to them that dwell on the earth, that they should make an image to the beast which had the wound by a sword, and did live.

Perilous times are coming, Saints of God; there is no power like God Almighty because He has all power in His hands. It is important that Christians pray together with Love and stand together. Stop fighting one another; we are going to need one another right now and when that mark of the beast comes on this earth

Revelation 13:18

Here is wisdom. Let him that hath understanding count the number of the beast: for it is the number of a man; and his number is Six hundred threescore and six.

Saints, the beast is going to be a man when that time comes. The man's number is going to be 666. But God will redeem His people from this earth. And if anyone takes that mark he will be an enemy to God.

Revelation 14:10-11

[10]The same shall drink of the wine of the wrath of God, which is poured out without mixture into the cup of His indignation; and he shall be tormented with fire and brimstone in the presence of the Lamb: [11]And the smoke of their torment ascendeth up for ever and ever: And they have no rest day or night, who worship the beast and his image, and whosoever receiveth the mark of his name."

We always say, when one of our Loved ones dies, that we will see them again. If they die in Christ Jesus and you have not given Christ your life, you won't see them again. If you are in Christ when you die, and they were not in Christ, you still won't see them. All must be born again.

Revelation 14:13

And I heard a voive from heaven saying unto me, Write, Blessed are dead which die in the Lord from henceforth: Yea, saith the spirit that they may rest from their labours; and their works do follow them.

It is time for every Preacher, Evangelist, Apostle, Bishop—everybody that God has chosen—to feed His sheep. It is time to preach the book of Revelation to His people. And if we don't obey God, the wrath comes on disobedient children. We have spent enough time talking about money and houses, and everything except teaching about souls being saved and the end time. People are sitting in church today who don't even know how important it is to be saved and about what's about to take place on this earth.

Whatever you all are preaching about now—Stop. Give the world the Revelation that is coming upon this earth. Homosexuals, adulterers, liars, false prophets, thieves—give them a chance to repent from their sins. They must know about the Lamb's book of life before Jesus comes back. We must tell them that Jesus Christ will save them from their sins.

"The Seven angels pour out the seven bowls of God's wrath"

Revelation 16:2-4

[2]The first went, and poured out his vial upon the earth; and there fell a noisome and grievous sore

upon the men which had the mark of the beast, and upon them which worshipped his image.

[3]And the second angel poured out his vial upon the sea; and it became as blood of a dead man: and every living soul died in the sea.

[4]And the third angel poured out his vial upon the rivers and fountains of waters: and they because blood.

Revelation 16:8

And the fourth angel poured out his vial upon the sun; and power was given unto him to scorch men with fire.

Revelation 16:10

And the fifth angel poured out his vial upon the seat of the beast; and the kingdom was full of darkness; and they gnawed their tongues for pain.

Revelation 16:12

And the sixth angel poured out his vial upon the great river, Euphrates; and the water thereof was dried up that the way of there of the east might be prepared.

Revelation 16:17

And the seventh angel poured out his vial into the air: and there came out a voice out of the temple of Heaven, from the throne, saying It is done.

What a day it will be when Christ comes back for His own. "Christ coming on a white horse." He is *king of kings and lord of lords.* The beast and the false prophets are cast alive into the lake of fire. "Burning with brimstone. And there will be judgment at the great white Throne." There will be two books.

Because there will be a new heaven, a new earth and a New Jerusalem.

Revelation 21:4-5

[4]And God shall wipe away all tears from their eyes; and there shall be no more death, neither sorrow, nor crying, neither shall there be any more pain: for the former things are passed away.
[5]And He that sat upon the throne said, behold, I make all things new. And He said unto me, Write: for these words are true and faithful.

Revelation 21:8

But the fearful, and unbelieving, and the abominable, and murderers, and whoremongers, and sorcerers, and idolaters, and all liars, shall have their part in the lake which burneth with fire and brimstone: which is the second death.

It will be all worth fighting for, that Great City that God has prepared for us. The Bible tells us that the city has twelve gates, and that the gates are pure gold like clean glass. And the walls are like precious stone; the streets are pure gold as it were transparent glass. In that city we won't need any sun, or the moon to shine. The Glory of God will lighten it. And there shall be no night in that city.

Revelation 21:24

And the nation of them which are saved shall walk in the light of it: and the kings of the earth do their glory and honor into it.

Revelation 21:27

And there shall in no wise enter into it any thing that defileth, neither neither whatsoever worketh abomination, or maketh a lie: but they which are written in the Lamb's book of life.

Revelation 22:5

And there shall be no more night there: and they need no candle, neither light of the sun; for the Lord God given them light and they shall reign for ever and ever.

The return of the Lord Jesus Christ:

Revelation 22:7

Behold, I come quickly: blessed is he that keepth the saying of the prophecy of this book.

Revelation 22:10

And He saith unto me, Seal not the saying of the prophecy of this book: for the time is at hand.

Revelation 22:11

He that is unjust let him be let him be unjust still: and he which is filthy, let him be filthy still: and he that is righteous, let him be righteous still: and he that is holy, let him be holy still.

Revelation 22:13

I am Alpha and Omega, the beginning and the end,
the first and the last.

God said they that keep His comments will have the right to the tree of Life, that we may enter into the gates and the city that He has prepared for us, that whosoever will let Him come.

Why do you think that the enemy doesn't want men and women, boys and girls to know about the Book of Life? It's because he wants to destroy everybody He can, to take them with him to hell, and to keep them from knowing Jesus. God has chosen His people to stand for the truth.

Revelation 22:19

And if any man shall take away from the words of the book of this prophecy. God shall take away his part out of the book of Life, and out of the holy city and from the things which are written in this book.

I used to hear the older Saints say, "Everything going down but the word of God." That is so true because God is good. Believer and unbeliever, it's time out for playing church. The end is near. I used to hear the older Saints sing that song, *I want to go to that city*, and then they would sing, *In that city over there. In that city.*

Knowing what is about to take place on this earth, yes, I want to go to that city.

> "God works though the lives of people to accomplish His desires. Earthy Kingdoms may rise and fall, but God and His word will last forever. If we will commit ourselves to God, good will triumph over evil in our lives. God is concerned about every area of our lives even our diets and eating habits. Only God knows all, sees all and hears all, and thus only He is worthy of Lord of our lives."
>
> (Holman Rainbow Study Bible)

God will give us wisdom if we only ask him. The Bible says man "shall not live by bread alone, but my every word of God." In these last days we are going to have to fast, for more of God's wisdom, to be able to stand in these last days. Wisdom and might belong to God and all things are his. Thank Him for the wisdom and understanding; there will be a time when the Saints are going to have to stand together as one with God. There will be a time when we may have to trust God, or face death.

Love Them Enough to Pull Them out of the Fire

Romans 8:35

Who shall separate us from the love of Christ? Shall tribulation, or distress, or peril, or sword?

On the day of Revelation, you are going to have to stand on these words. Look at Daniel: trust God in God even if took him to lose his life in the fire. Daniel knew that God has all power. We, as Saints, must believe.

"Christianity is more than a religion it is a relationship with Jesus Christ. To be victorious, we must run the race with our eyes on Jesus. We can give our temptations to Jesus He has already faced all of them and won the victory. God desires His children to give strength of testimony to each other. Only the blood of Christ can cleanse us of our sins."

(Holman Rainbow Study Bible)

Romans 8:28

And we know that all things work together for good to them that Love God, to them who are the called according to His purpose.

Romans 8:31

What shall we then say to these things. If God be for us, who can be against us?

There is power in God's Love, because Love is power from on high. Whenever you need help standing up, stand on these words of God.

Matthew 12:25-26

²⁵And Jesus knew their thoughts, and said unto them, every kingdom divided against itself is brought to desolation; and every city or house divided against itself shall not stand.

²⁶And if Satan cast out Satan he is divided against himself: how shall then His kingdom stand?

Matthew 12:28

But if I cast out devils by the Spirit of God, then the kingdom of God is come unto you.

Chapter 9: Daily Prayers

Day One Prayer:

Dear Lord, you allow me to be able to walk, talk, and see another day .I just want to thank and give you a "Hallelujah!" praise for that. Also, clear Lord, I want you to help me to love like Jesus loves. And do the vineyard work like Jesus did, ever if I have to go by myself.

Amen!

Day Two Prayer:

Lord Jesus I come to you with thankgsgiving and praise.

I know I need your help dear Lord, help me to live this life free from sin.

I ask you today to forgive me of my sins,

And give me a clean heart and mind. A heart for you,

Amen!

Day Three Prayer:

Dear Lord, I want to thank you for another day. I have never seen this day before, dear Lord, and I want to do something I have never done before. I want you to guide me and give me the truth.
Amen!

Day Four Prayer:

Dear Lord, I come to you with thanksgiving, thanking you for being so good.
Thank you for being God, the true in living. I'm asking you to order my steps this day, to guide me in your prefect way.
I ask you to help keep me humble, with your love.
Amen!

Day Five Prayer:

I come to you with a praise, because you are worthy.
I am thanking you for all you have done or me in my life.
Thank you for keeping me, and I know now that there is nothing too hard for my Lord.
Thank you.
Amen!

Day Six Prayer:

Dear Lord, I just want to take time to thank you,

and you Son ,Jesus Christ. Father God, I come to you as a chosen pastor, chosen by God asking you to help me to feed your sheep's the way you command me to do.

To help me Guide them out, into your vineyard for your work.

The harvest is plentiful but the labourers, are few.

I ask you to put me on the move for God and His vineyard work before Jesus returns.

Amen!

Acknowledgments

Proverbs 22:6

Train up a child in the way he should go: and when he gets old, he will not depart from it.

This book that God has allowed me to write is possible because of the way my Father and Mother brought me up. They always prayed for me regularly and encouraged me each day. I would like to think God for Willie and Bernice Woodard.

Their faithfulness and dedication to God is why I'm writing this book today. It's important to know Jesus Christ, and to have a relationship with him, so I ask God to use this book to help other who don't know Jesus Christ to get know Him.

I also ask God to encourage the Saints, that the vineyard work and in the street ministry is very much need.

Love Them Enough to Pull Them out of the Fire

Matthew 9:37

Then saith He unto His disciples, the harvest truly is plenteous, but the laboures are few."

Made in the USA
Middletown, DE
27 May 2017